a portrait of

MADRAS COLLEGE

Photography	Peter Adamson
Editor	Lorn Macintyre
Designer	Jon Gill

First published in Great Britain in 2011 by
Madras College
St Andrews, Fife KY16 9EJ
www.madras.fife.sch.uk

Design by Jon Gill
jongill.co.uk

Printed and bound in Great Britain by
Winter & Simpson Dundee
www.wintersimpson.co.uk

ISBN 978-0-9570237-0-3

A   P O R T R A I T   O F

Acknowledgements

I am grateful to the following for their generous financial support:
David Evans (former pupil).
Murray Donald Drummond Cook.
Pagan Osborne.
Fife Council.
Madras College Endowment Trust.
St Andrews Community Trust.
Henderson Black & Co.

Many pupils, members of staff and former pupils have written articles or captions. I thank them for their contribution to the book. Special thanks are due to Emma Sunter who took it upon herself to liaise with Peter Adamson over the many events and activities that he photographed; to Lindsay Matheson for his contributions to the archive; to Colin Blake without whose willing cooperation many of the photographs would not have been possible. Morag Wilson, our Admin Coordinator in the Madras office, has been so helpful and patient in assisting in the preparation of this book for the press. Without doubt, Peter Adamson's keen eye, enthusiasm and determination have all contributed to the wonderful photographs he has taken. We will always be in his debt for producing this unique record, a year in the life of Madras College. I am equally grateful to Lorn Macintyre for his skill as editor in merging pictures and text.

Ian Jones, Rector.

FOREWORD
Ian Jones, Rector

4

'The rather austere bust of Rev Dr Andrew Bell is an ever-present reminder of the unique history of Madras College which, with the construction of a new school, is about to begin a new chapter. At the end of the third term each year we hold a Great Assembly in Holy Trinity Church at which we celebrate Easter, we recognise the legacy of Andrew Bell and we appreciate the talents of our own pupils. In thinking about Andrew Bell we recognise:

- his establishment of Madras College by his own generosity,
- his desire to improve learning for all pupils by using every technique possible apart from corporal punishment,
- his important idea and principle that we often learn best when we learn from each other,
- his modern theory that learning is done best in small steps,
- the thousands of pupils who are proud to have gone before us through this school,
- the millions worldwide who have benefited from Bell's ideas,
- the value of having high standards, being positive and giving each other support,
- the need every so often to dedicate ourselves to renewed effort to do our best for ourselves and for others.

Andrew Bell was quite fixed in his ideas and single-minded. He did not seek easy popularity. However, he made his mark in difficult and changing times. He gained great respect from the pupils he taught, and he contributed to the improvement of education for the whole of society. To have him as our founder gives us a unique heritage, and challenges us to study and apply some of his ideas in the 21st century. By reflecting on our past we can learn much and understand what Madras College is aiming to achieve for everyone, how personal ambition and mutual support can go hand in hand, and how having a clear set of values is vital for a healthy school or society. For all of these things we have reason to be grateful to Andrew Bell.'

The Story of Madras College from 1833

Madras College was founded in 1833, following a bequest by the eminent educational reformer Dr Andrew Bell, himself a native of the town. Born in St Andrews on 27th March 1753, he was educated in the town grammar school and university before seeking fame and fortune in the British colony of Virginia. There he made money in the lucrative tobacco trade and also as tutor to the sons of Carter Braxton, a leading light of the rebellion against British rule and one of the signatories of the American Declaration of Independence. When he returned to Britain in 1781 he embarked on an entirely different career, becoming ordained as an Episcopalian minister and taking charge of the chapel in Leith in 1785. Still restless, however, he set out two years later to India, where he intended making money in Calcutta from illustrated lectures on science. Stopping on the way in Madras (South India), he gave some lectures and became a local celebrity, accepting posts as chaplain to various regiments and - significantly for us - running the Male Military Asylum, a school for orphans. It was there that he first had the idea of his Madras System of education, in which he believed the most worthwhile system of elementary education was one based on what he called the "principles of mutual instruction." He devoted the remainder of his life to spreading this system far and wide. Andrew Bell founded, or supervised the foundation of an extraordinary number of British schools during the first three decades of the nineteenth century. Under his scheme, which he personally supervised with extreme rigour in hundreds of his schools, those pupils who had mastered a lesson or part of a lesson would instruct their peers. This reduced the number of teachers required to carry out good learning to the extent that one master could be responsible for a hundred pupils or more. It worked best with the rudiments of learning such as writing, spelling, reading and arithmetic. Bell was more than anyone responsible for the concept of monitorial education and pupil-teachers. He also believed in recording misdemeanours in a "black book" and was against the use of corporal punishment.

It was Andrew Bell's vision that his final foundation should also be his finest, and should apply the "principles of mutual instruction" to elementary and more advanced studies in a new school for the whole community of St Andrews. The new institution subsumed the two main existing schools of the time, the long-established Grammar School and the more recent English School (in which Latin was not taught), and was governed for its first 66 years by a board of trustees drawn from the civic and the university authorities. There were four departments in the early days, each levying small termly fees for instruction. Considerable numbers of pupils from home and abroad boarded while studying. Some boarders stayed within the school premises, while others found lodgings in the many independent boarding establishments which grew up in the town. It appears that Bell's hopes in respect of applying his principles of "mutual instruction" to secondary education were never fully realised, and that the style of education received was not dissimilar to that of other institutions of the time.

Following the Education Act of 1886 the Burgh School was established, providing free secondary education to the age of 14, so that the schools existed in parallel, each with its associated primary schools. The first rector of Madras College was appointed in 1889 by the Board of Governors which had replaced the Trustees. During World War One the school was used as an artillery training centre. In 1926 the school's independent existence ended when it was taken over by Fife County Council. After World War Two the catchments of both Madras College and the Burgh School widened, the secondary departments of Guardbridge, Leuchars and Newport being brought within the Burgh School in 1957. Following the national decision to extend "comprehensive" education the two schools were reunited in 1963, using two campuses, Kilrymont Road for juniors, and South Street for seniors. One modern reminder of Bell's "principles of mutual instruction" is still to be found in the practice of "peer tutoring," in which over one hundred senior pupils normally devote a proportion of their weekly timetable to assisting junior pupils in their studies. In 1999 the school roll rose to a maximum of 1850. Following lengthy negotiations between Fife Council and the University of St Andrews, it was decided in 2009 that a new single-campus Madras College should be built.

Our school has a distinctive and colourful story to tell, reflecting the historical period of its foundation; the individuals who made their mark on its character and style; the particular features and traditions that emerged; the sentiments of appreciation and loyalty it fostered; and the record of service to pupils and the community it achieved. Our purpose in this book is to give life and meaning to this story by capturing the breadth and variety of a single year in the 178 year story of Madras College.

Lindsay Matheson, Rector,
Madras College, 1997-2007.

'It was a weird sensation walking into my first proper Castle House assembly. My Primary 1 memories came rushing back to me. It was daunting walking through the doors with all the older kids looking down on you. It was a new learning experience.'

B*en Hasselgren, S1.*

Next page: First day at Kilrymont Road in August 2011.

THE OLD ORDER CHANGETH

This page: A detail from the plaque presented on the previous page.

Previous page: 'The bas relief, *top left*, is a bronze copy of a section of Dr Andrew Bell's tomb in Westminster Abbey. It depicts him observing children "giving the lesson" to each other as his system dictated. This is in the same section of the Madras College building as the coat of arms and THE OLD ORDER CHANGETH.'

'The bronze plaque, *bottom left,* is the school's coat of arms with the three "Bells" (no coincidence!). The location is near the south-west corner of the original quadrangle, where the link was formed to the first major extension to the 1833 building, completed in 1955 at the end of Dr Macleod's time. THE OLD ORDER CHANGETH (a phrase of Alfred Lord Tennyson's) was cut in the stone to mark this change. The location is a favourite for pupils to have their photographs taken as souvenirs; indeed the location is simply known as The old order changeth'!

Lindsay Matheson, Rector, 1997-2007.

'We shape our buildings; thereafter they shape us.'

Winston Churchill, 1943.

12

'The Celtic Block, so named because it was once painted green, is the tallest of the buildings at the South Street site. Two narrow staircases spiral to the top of the building, a gruelling climb, especially on a Monday morning. With views all around St Andrews this building is a key part of South Street.

Despite the Celtic Block being one building it has a variety of uses. It houses workshops, kitchens, labs and the Guidance base. This leads to a complex array of sounds and smells, from the racket of a band-saw to the bangs and pops of the Chemistry lab, or the smell of a chemical reaction to the sweet smell of fresh baking.

The Celtic Block is just one of the many buildings that make up South Street, and every pupil at Madras will leave with some memories of it, be they from excelling in science or learning to cook. The Celtic Block is a great example of what Madras College is all about - a diverse group of skills and subjects being taught to an even wider variety of pupils.'

David Ford, S6.

Dr Andrew Bell, begetter of Madras College, keeps a benign eye on present-day pupils from the sanctuary of an enclosure on the stairs.

'I was very friendly with Ian Stewart, the architect and designer of the Kilrymont Road building of Madras College. During a conversation regarding the design I made a remark about the "Chinese pagodas" of the dining hall, the Music Department and the Technical Department. Ian said to me that if I went further down the games field I would see (using my imagination) that the design represented seagulls flying towards the cliffs (the main building).

Looking towards the west, the outline of the Physical Education Department is also unusual - that of a bomber sitting on the tarmac at Leuchars. During a lovely summer evening the silhouette reflects the rays of the sun as the material used is hammered aluminium.'

Keith Neilson, former Madras pupil (1943-49), and Deputy Principal Teacher of Physical Education at Madras (1964-86).

'Some staff choose to cycle between South St and Kilrymont Rd - which can be unpleasant if the weather is typically Scottish! Here I am taking some light exercise "between buildings."'

Billy Macmillan, Chemistry.

The super-efficient office staff of Madras is on the ball. The team, back row, left to right: Shelagh Docherty; Val Weir; Elizabeth Austin; Carole Cameron; Mary Milne. Morag Wilson kneels, keeping the score; Donna Montador (also kneeling), keeps an eye on the clock; on the chair, Rona Robertson; and behind her, having thrown the pass, Carol Harrower.

This team of ladies will tackle anything!

'As school janitor, covering a large area of buildings, I have to make sure that the bell is rung each day at precisely 8.42am and 13.37pm - odd times you might think, but this is a warning bell for pupils, allowing them just enough time to be sitting down in their classrooms before lessons begin three minutes later. As I pull the rope, I like to see the kids jump into action. The original bell, housed in the east tower, would have been used in the pre-electronic age.'

Colin Blake, school janitor.

Keeping Madras running smoothly -
clockwise, top left: printing, correcting, lunching, socialising.

'Who really knows what School Technicians do... pupils? No, they don't know. Teachers? Yes, they know what help they receive within their department. Management? Hmmm yes, they admit that the Technicians do a 'grand job'.... Read on if you want to know...

Electrical equipment - provide a testing and repair service.

IT – install and repair all computers and associated devices.

Science – make up and maintain all kits and set up experiments throughout years 1 – 6.

Craft & Design – maintain all machines and cut wood as per cutting lists.'

Front: Brian Blacklaw, Senior Technician, writer of above. Back, left to right: Eric Box; Andrew Fyall; John Love.

'With no super-injunctions to gag us, we amateur newshounds went fearlessly in search of the latest scoops at Madras College. Our articles and photographs reporting events such as school exchanges, trips, fundraisers and Royal visits appeared fortnightly as a Madras Diary in the St. Andrews Citizen. Without resorting to phone hacking, we provided readers with a small insight into life at Madras. Eat your heart out Rupert Murdoch!

Back half of the circle, left to right: Mark Nicoll; Natalie Crawford; Rachel Wilson; Lauren Russell. Nearest to the camera, left to right: Thea Blackadder; Emma Sunter; Lindsay Wright; Andrew Johnston.'

Emma Sunter, S6.

A PORTRAIT OF

A   P O R T R A I T   O F

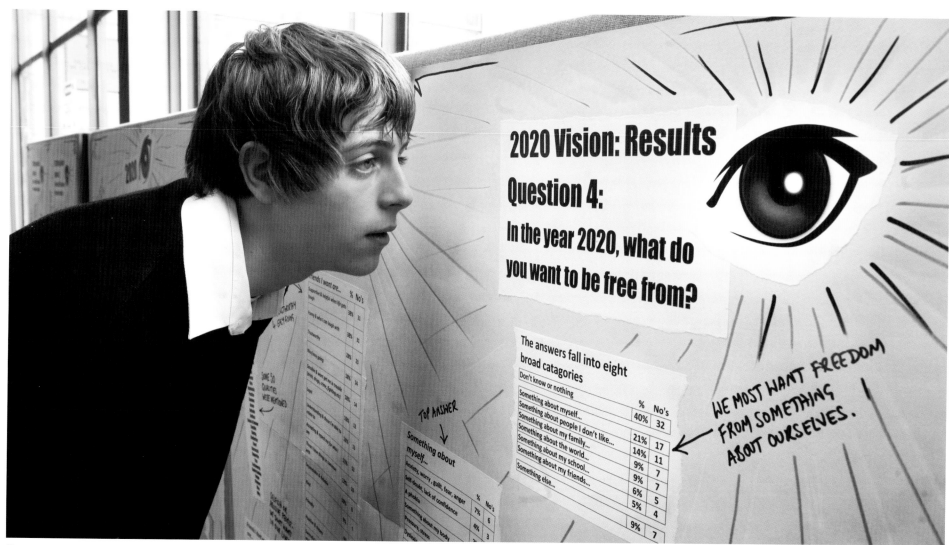

'I was interested in the hypnotic eye drawing me in; then, looking closer, I noticed writing: "In the year 2020, what do you want to be free from?" I went away and thought about the question for a while. When I returned I replied: "Nothing really!"'

Lui Watters, S3.

MADRAS COLLEGE

27

'Madras College won an "Awards for All" grant and bought 15 quality mountain bikes, with all safety accessories, and a bike trailer. With trained staff, pupils in all age groups from S1-S6 are offered the opportunity to use these bikes to improve bike handling skills and to encourage cycling as a healthy lifestyle option.

Pupils learn basic bike check procedures and are taught riding skills and techniques in the school environment. Groups progress onto roads and identify safe routes, with senior classes cycling on more challenging trails in Tentsmuir Forest or Kingsbarns.

The picture shows *Wes Reid* in S1 demonstrating one of the more advanced skills!'

Jim Tarvet, PE Teacher.

'S4 pupils are given the opportunity to learn bicycle maintenance as part of a Business Enterprise. The main aims of the maintenance course are to encourage young people's interest in cycling for pleasure, to explore the local countryside and to learn the practical skills associated with keeping their own bicycles in good running order.'

Gavin Waterston, Department of Additional Support.

A PORTRAIT OF

'Business Education and Computing came together under one faculty in 2005 and is now managed by one Curriculum Leader, myself, *Julie McLaren*. I have a background in both subject areas. *From left: Magnus Latona; Janice Paterson; Keith Maskell; Julie McLaren; Stephen Forbes; Alice Little.*

"It's chic to be geek!" Over the years, the computer scientists of the faculty have striven to be at the forefront of computer technologies, whilst the entrepreneurs of Business Education keep abreast of developments in business management, finance and marketing.'

Julie McLaren, Curriculum Leader, Business Education and Computing.

'Computing Studies in Madras College enable pupils to gain extensive computer skills which prove very beneficial, both in future employment and further education. The photograph shows 4th year Standard Grade pupils hard at work with their programming assessments.'

Keith Maskell, teacher of Computing.

A PORTRAIT OF

Modern technology allows a pupil to turn herself into a film director, though the cast she has lined up looks a bit cowed.

A P O R T R A I T O F

'The PE Department this year have taught table tennis, badminton, handball, softball, water-polo, volleyball, basketball, tennis, beach-volleyball, mountain biking, contemporary dance, orienteering and kite-flying in addition to the traditional sports! Modern PE also offers certificate courses which allow pupils to gain qualifications, allowing them to fully develop their sporting potential. Some staff still volunteer to take after-school sports clubs as well as participating in inter-school fixtures.'

Malcolm Changleng, Principal Teacher (Curriculum), Physical Education.

During session 2010-2011 the Madras basketball teams were busy, playing other Fife schools at S4 level, and the senior boys' team competed in the Scottish Cup, finishing top equal in its group. Coaches Donald Grewar and Vikki Birmingham have thoroughly enjoyed working with the boys, and look forward to a successful second year in 2011-2012. There is also mention of a girls' team starting up next year.

'The all-weather surface at Kilrymont is an excellent area on which to hone our hockey skills. Grass pitches are too inconsistent and the ball often "bobbles" up. I enjoyed this lesson with *Mr McLuskie* because he teaches us through playing fun practices, but he also hammers home the basics of the sport.'

*R*oss Cunningham, S1.

Previous page: 'The Madras Kilrymont Sports Hall is spacious, but badly designed because the roof slopes down sharply. This means that games players often hit the low roof with their shuttlecocks, volleyballs etc.'

*M*alcolm Changleng, *Principal Teacher, Physical Education.*

A PORTRAIT OF

'The celebrated success of Madras College's senior rugby team in past years has been clear and prominent throughout my six years at the school. Witnessing several of Madras's victories and experiencing them first hand as a player, has confirmed the recognition of Madras as the leading rugby playing school in the area. Being a member of this team gives me pleasure and enjoyment, not only from playing the game and being a part of the traditions, but also by being immersed in the social community that is generated. The role of Captain at a school such as Madras has given me honour, pride and memories I will never forget!'

Ciaran Hynd, S6, 1st XV rugby Captain.

'This is Madras playing Buckhaven in a league match which we won 4-1. *Jordan Davidson* (Vice-Captain and central defender) is heading a clearance away from a Buckhaven corner kick. *Daniel Hart* (Captain) is in goal. Madras went on to become Fife Schools Under 18 Champions.'

Harvey Munn, Physical Education.

The Science Department, *left to right*: Peter Tomb (Principal Teacher, Curriculum); Bill Kilgour; Graham Reid; Rachel Gray; Fiona Paterson; Sean Duffy; David Paton; Billy Macmillan; Marion Glancy; David Crone; Brendan Fox; Patricia McIntyre.

A PORTRAIT OF

MADRAS COLLEGE

'The Bell Pettigrew Museum offered a unique learning experience outside of the classroom, which proved enjoyable for the members of the Advanced Higher Biology class. The Museum, situated in St Andrews is small, yet brimming with a variety of organisms from all continents, demonstrating the diversity of life on our planet. The displays illustrated the subtle differences between species which make them perfectly suited to their environments, allowing us to appreciate the significance of natural selection and to deepen our understanding of the process of evolution. Furthermore, it enabled us to see how animals are classified and ordered by taxonomists. Overall, the Museum makes a memorable and beneficial experience for anyone passionate about biology.'

Hannah Leech, S6, ruminating beside skull.

The Light Fantastic: *Lucy Harrower and Sam Johnson, S3* are mesmerized by the refraction of light. This is when light bends as it passes at a slant through an interface between two materials. It is a phenomenon familiar to fishermen, who see their fishing lines appear to bend in the water. This set-up shows us how light refracts when it enters our eyes, and how an image is created on the back of our retina.

'A van de graaf using a belt to collect charges that are electro-statically stable and are collected on the hollow globe at the top. One person stands on an insulator to prevent electric shocks. As the belt collects the charges they build up in us and try to escape, causing our hair to stand up on end. This is a fun experiment that shows us how electric fields act and what they look like.'

Freja Connell and James Picken, S3.

A PORTRAIT OF

'My favourite part of chemistry is experiments. I love them, especially ones with bunsens. My favourite one so far has been combusting magnesium in the flame, though you shouldn't look directly at the burning magnesium, due to the intensity of light emitted. It's interesting to see the effect the heat has on magnesium and other elements. The burning magnesium was used in flares and flash bulbs.'

Calum McDonald, S3 (on left).

'My favourite part of chemistry is the experiments. My favourite experiment is burning substances to find the colour given off, as shown in the photograph.'

Robbie Sharp, S3 (on right).

'I'm Cameron Ward and I was playing Joe Greig in an investigative drama The Other Side of the Wall, written and devised by my Higher class. We were exploring issues of private versus public school education. I am playing a working class, recently made unemployed father in the photo. In this play I am trying to reassure my son, Junior (*Liam Vincent-Kilbride*) and guide him in his young school career. I didn't want him to make the same mistakes as me and leave school without any qualifications.

Drama is a fantastic subject which has allowed me to bloom with confidence throughout my school life and personal life. It has given me the belief to strive for better opportunities and to raise my targets in the near future.'

Cameron Ward, S5 (left).

'Madras College English Department is headed up by me, Olav Darge, Principal Teacher. The Department consists of 14 members of staff, some of whom are missing from this photograph. This pose lasted for around 10 minutes, after which staff had to flee to Kilrymont to take their next class.

Occasionally classes are held in the Quad on sunny days, when acting out a play, or looking for inspiration for writing, or even as a quiet place to read, or perhaps because they are just a little bit annoying...where pupils can sit in their own pew.

Left to right, back row: two standing on chairs - Jason Hynes; Neil Baillie. Middle row: Vicki Birmingham; Dorothy Comber; Ian Boyd; Julia Matthews. Sitting on chairs: Olav Darge; Emma Payne. On ground: Annwen Griffiths.

The Letters being held by teachers require no explanation for "Countdown" viewers.'

O*lav Darge, Principal Teacher of English.*

Opposite: Higher English: studies in concentration for a vital examination.

Autumn

*Where it's nearly Christmas but
not quite*

*Not quite bitterly cold but the
sun no longer shines.*

*Hurried dashes through pelting
droplets of rain*

*Kicking up a dancing cloud of
leaves in russet tones.*

*Faces obscured by bright woollen
hats and scarves*

*People clutch smooth mahogany
conkers in gloved hands.*

*Nights grow steadily darker as
days pass by,*

*fingers of black creep stealthily
through the pale sky.*

*Water seems to burn numb
freezing fingers,*

*Plants adorned with silver
sparkles of frost.*

*The fleeting period when breezy
summer is chased away*

*but the twinkle of Christmas
spirit is not quite here*

The turning point of the year.

Lauren Galloway, S3.

The Rector and his deputies, *left to right*:
Lisa Grubb; John Urquhart; Ann Adamson; Ian
Jones (Rector); Lynsey Seeley;
Colin Mackay; Barry Millar.

Remembrance Day, 11 November 2011.
'It is easy to take liberty for granted, when you have never had it taken from you.'
Dick Cheney, United States Vice-President, 2001-2009.

'I was honoured when I was asked to play the pipes at the Remembrance Day Service. It was a great privilege to be able to pay my respects through piping to those who died fighting for our country. A large number of teachers and pupils turned out to pay their respects.'

Connor Burgess, S5.

'Jock Steven is one of the many successful former pupils from Madras College to make a return visit. As we chatted, he modestly told me that it was in this very classroom Miss Ferguson tried in vain to teach him to speak fluent French. Luckily, this did not hold him back in later life. Since captaining the Junior School rugby team from 1949 to 1951 he has been greatly involved with rugby. He took part in Scottish matches against Ireland and France before becoming President of the Scottish Rugby Union from 1993-1994. Très bien, Monsieur Steven!'

Emma Sunter, S6, recipient of the Rector's Prize at the prize giving ceremony on 16 June 2011.

A PORTRAIT OF

An unusual perspective, from Madras College grounds, of the surviving north transept of the 16th century Dominican convent church of Blackfriars, reputed to have been the first building vandalised in the Reformation, a reminder to Madras pupils studying history of the violence and desecration in the story of St Andrews.

'When leaving the Kilrymont Road building on 16th December 2010, having taken photographs of the S1 Christmas Dance, I was intrigued by the ghostly reflections in the puddles of the artificially illuminated trees and school. Aware that the lawn in the foreground was deep in shadow, I positioned my car to allow the twin beams of light to add detail to the scene, sufficient for a photographic exposure. This is what I saw.'

Peter Adamson, photographer.

A   P O R T R A I T   O F

'In photography, the smallest thing can become a great subject. The little human detail can become a leitmotiv.'

Henri Cartier-Bresson, the father of photo-journalism.

The Mathematics Department staff, *left to right:* Tom Inglis; Alastair Cuthbertson; Craig Trewartha; Laura O'Donnell; Carol Neilson, Principal Teacher; Donald Grewar; Susan Grant; Alison Massie; Sandy Farmer; Peter Ross.

'One Monday Kayleigh and I arrived at Maths room 318. Mr Gourlay came in and said: "would you all like to be in a picture with my wife and my twins Manny and Abby?" Some of us said yes and some of us said no. I felt excited about this as I would get my picture taken with little twins. Mr Gourlay got us together for a group photo which is now going to be in the school book.'

Emma Russell and Kayleigh Thompson, S1.

A PORTRAIT OF

Protracted calculations in a Maths class to get an angle on the subject.

A swinging time at the S1 dance in mid December, with the young man on the right evidently jiving in his own world.

A PORTRAIT OF

'The boy in the glow spectacles I was dancing with at the Christmas Party is just a mate. He was sitting beside me and I asked him if he would like to dance. He said: "OK." He wasn't a bad dancer, though!'

Georgie Kermode, S1.

A PORTRAIT OF

A PORTRAIT OF

'Bright lights, neon colours, roaring music! The oldies and the newbies and hundreds of school kids dancing together, all celebrating in the wonderful atmosphere of being young and free... nothing can come between old friends, new friends and good friends in the wholesome atmosphere of good, honest fun.'

Luanna Wilson, S6.

MADRAS COLLEGE

'Believe it or not this lot is in charge of educating your children! Now the Over Twenty Group certainly applies to our age as you can see but it is deeper than that…these staff are some of those who have been teaching at Madras for over twenty years with yours truly clocking up a magnificent 37 years man and boy!

We are a pleasant bunch of folk who need to have a bit of fun now and again and Peter captured us at one of these moments before the Christmas Party Season.

As you can imagine it is an exclusive club and younger staff can't wait to join our happy throng but I bet you can't recognise the prostrate teacher in the front!!!'

Colin Mackay, Depute Rector, venerated English teacher (retired July 2011).

Better than School

The darkening sky is interrupted by
A drifting sparkle, then another and another
Floating down, and when the night is black
A million frosty puffs furiously falling

Is school on? Unsure, wondering…
The confirmation of freedom like an unexpected gift
Parents working inside, daughter freezing in the garden
Three year old smiles and icy starfish hands
Helpless laughter as I stand covered in snow

Days go by, the hill's too dangerous.
We're all hungry, stop complaining.
This single never-ending white day
Is losing its novelty
But, it's better than school.
I wouldn't mind having a snow week next year!

Rosie Watt, S3.

A PORTRAIT OF

Look round and round upon this bare bleak plain, and see even here, upon a winter's day, how beautiful the shadows are! Alas! it is the nature of their kind to be so. The loveliest things in life, Tom, are but shadows; and they come and go, and change and fade away, as rapidly as these!

Charles Dickens, Martin Chuzzlewit.

A PORTRAIT OF

In any case life is but a procession of shadows, and God knows why it is that we embrace them so eagerly, and see them depart with such anguish, being shadows.

Virginia Woolf, Jacob's Room.

'Just as the school year unfolds, so are the changing seasons reflected in the appearance of the grounds of the school. After the pupils return to their studies while the summer sun is still shining, all too soon the trees unveil their autumnal colours. Winter can give us a beautiful blanket of white through which pupils must trudge to the warmth of their classrooms, often arriving and leaving in darkness, with hands deep in the pockets of their heavy winter coats. Spring sees the appearance of carpets of crocuses at South Street, quickly followed by the nodding heads of the yellow daffodils at Kilrymont. Summer is a very different affair, winter coats substituted by shirts, with their sleeves rolled up. Trees and flowers are at their peak, particularly the eye-catching blossom of the cherry trees lining the path to Kilrymont's front door, and the magnificence of South Street's chestnut tree standing in the long shadows of the ancient buildings.'

Jamie MacLeod, S2.

Opposite: Madras College Pipe Band blow and beat out appropriate tunes at a Burns Supper to an appreciative audience.

'You can keep the Prefectship and the House Captaincy; truly no position could instil a pupil with a greater sense of power and authority than that of bass drummer in the Madras College Pipe Band. There is simply nothing like kicking into a rendition of "The Black Bear" at one of the many prestigious events at which the band has the privilege of performing, or rather, the events which have had the privilege of the band's performances. These have included the Royal Wedding celebrations in St. Salvator's Quadrangle; the Dunhill Links Championship and the University of St. Andrews Alumni Ball.'

*Tommy Alexander,
bass drummer, S5.*

'The Burns Supper is an evening of good food (as long as you don't think about some of the ingredients), washed down with a drop of the hard stuff (Irn Bru); great Scottish music; riveting speeches and some first-rate poetry by Robert Burns (you've no idea what he's talking about but it's moving nonetheless).'

Alan Sunter, S4.

This page and next: Non-Uniform Day. An opportunity to relax in one's own gear.

Opposite: 'In a very real sense, people who have read good literature have lived more than people who cannot or will not read. It is not true that we have only one life to lead; if we can read, we can live as many more lives and as many kinds of lives as we wish.'

S.I. Hayakawa (1906-1992), academic and United States Senator.

'What a school thinks about its library is a measure of what it thinks about education.'

Harold Howe, former United States Commissioner of Education.

Right: the dining hall at Kilrymont that has catered for several generations of pupils.

'Although our involvement in debating has forced us to endure six years of casual bullying, it really wasn't all bad. We've met some interesting characters (including our tea-loving mentor Ed) and debated some ridiculous motions ("THW make UK companies producing in China contribute to carbon offsetting"). We've been in about 32 rounds in 15 competitions, hopefully gained a few brain cells, and definitely gained about 7000 calories from eating cakes, but we wouldn't have had it any other way.'

Katie O'Donnell, S6.

The Prefects and House Captains for the academic year 2011-12 muster for the camera.

'Skills Development Scotland is responsible for careers advice across Scotland. Career Advisers support pupils and parents with advice on career management skills, subject choice and options beyond school. In a time of recession, it is crucial that pupils make informed and realistic decisions. The jobs market and places at universities and colleges have become increasingly competitive. Pupils need to fully research future choices, with skills and personal strengths taken into account when planning for the future.

The Careers Base in South Street has a dedicated interview facility and careers library with internet access.'

Chris Simpson, Careers Service (with Cameron Tait, S6).

'The Talent Show was a terrific experience for everyone involved, from the participants to the 500+ audience members; and none more so than for my sister, Erin, who I accompanied on the guitar. This was going to be Erin's first time on stage, proving to the world what she could do and so, understandably, she was nervous. Within seconds, however, something changed. All of a sudden I noticed a new volume to her voice, a new shine to the song, and a confidence within her that I'd never before known. By the end of the song, I knew I had a sister different to when the first few chords were played. This for me is what the Talent Show is all about – giving pupils the opportunity to become a performer in front of hundreds of supportive people. In the end Erin must have been alright, as together, we won the junior title!'

Hal Gillman Morrissey, S5.

A   P O R T R A I T   O F

The Home Economics staff make creative use of utensils.
Left to right: Morag McManus; Susan Hill; Maureen Kyle, Principal Teacher (Curriculum); Heather Nisbet at back; Wilma Steven; Audrey Grieve.

Mrs Kyle with her S3 Standard Grade Home Economics class, making pineapple upside down pudding. In Standard Grade the course consists of two periods of theory and one period where practical cookery skills are developed.

'The Techno Party was a relief when it came around, the sign that the Prelims had finished. The party was on Thursday 10th February and was organised by a group of S6. Everyone was looking forward to the night of dancing and music bursting out of speakers. What a great night it was! The music was full of energetic beats and the atmosphere was electric. Definitely worth the £3!'

Finlay McLean, S5.

A Visit From The Sea

Far from the loud sea beaches
Where he goes fishing and crying,
Here in the inland garden
Why is the sea-gull flying?

Here are no fish to dive for;
Here is the corn and lea;
Here are the green trees rustling.
Hie away home to sea!

Fresh is the river water
And quiet among the rushes;
This is no home for the sea-gull
But for the rooks and thrushes.

Pity the bird that has wandered!
Pity the sailor ashore!
Hurry him home to the ocean,
Let him come here no more!

High on the sea-cliff ledges
The white gulls are trooping and crying,
Here among the rooks and roses,
Why is the sea-gull flying?

*R*obert Louis Stevenson

'Is it a bird? Is it a plane? Is it... Superman? Yes! It's a seagull. The Expressive Arts faculty staff look for inspiration in the school quad and spot a lonely seagull on the roof. Immediately thoughts turn to how to use the image in a creative way. The dramatists think of Chekhov's seagull. Musicians consider sounds of the sea. Artists imagine lonely seascapes. Faculty staff always work together to promote a love of artistic expression in pupils. Creating, presenting and evaluating are the skills taught to all at school, often leading to performances, concerts and exhibitions for the wider community.'

Robin Dewar, Principal Teacher (Curriculum), Creative & Expressive Arts.

Front (recumbent), Jo Braggins. First row, left to right: Robin Dewar; Patricia Esler; Janice Nisbet. Second row: Ann Adamson; Roisin McGrath; Anne Stewart; Diane Houston. Third row, at back: Stephen Povey; Richard Wotherspoon; Alison Burns; Joanne Petrie.

A moment to reflect: Olivia Cannon, S6, explores self-portraiture on an enormous scale as part of her Advanced Higher Art course. She considers the questions: 'Who am I?' 'What do you see?' 'My alter ego?'

'Madras College Art Department has always produced a great quality of art work, spanning many different styles and mediums, including sculpture, jewellery design, textiles, graphic design, traditional paints and pastels and more. The excellent range of students who study the subject are encouraged to create work that is of personal interest to them, resulting in a wide range of extraordinary ideas and themes. This good work never goes unrewarded, as a sea of colour and ideas pours into the rest of the school from the Art Department's doors, showcasing the impressive work of the pupils on corridor walls and beyond.'

Ciaran Hynd, S6.

'I thought the art course throughout the year was lots of fun. We made many sculptures and drew lots of interesting art. I have really improved in my artwork from primary to first year and recommend any coming first year pupil to take art in secondary school.' *Alastair Jones, S1.*

'This is an unfinished picture of a friend. It is painted in acrylics and is about 75x100cms. I am interested in the relationship between appearance and reality and wanted to capture the sense of struggle beneath my friend's calm outer appearance. I painted the head and shoulders only so that I could concentrate on the principal expressive features of the face. The bold brush strokes, the angular eyebrows and the unkempt hair are an attempt to create a slightly aggressive rather than a traditionally beautiful portrait.'

Naomi Culpin, S6.

Previous page: 'I know I'm lucky to be learning piano at school with Mrs MacLeod. She picks music that I enjoy and it's great to play it in the assembly hall on the grand piano.'

Clodagh Ryan, S2.

'The Madras College Orchestra is a wonderful opportunity for pupils to develop their musical skills and meet new people. As a member since my second year, I have enjoyed the chance to play my violin as part of a group, and to hear the great sounds produced by the ensemble as a whole. We play a variety of music which challenges our individual abilities and we perform regularly at school and local events.'

Rory Lamb, S5 (extreme left) who plays violin in the school's Senior Strings.

A PORTRAIT OF

'I play violin and bagpipes. It's great fun to play in groups (I play in the fiddle group and the pipe band) and on your own. I like playing Scottish music. Learning music is good because it's a break from normal classes. It gives you new skills and it's not competitive.'

Hamish Ballantyne, S1.

'When it was announced that I had come first in the Fife Championships, I could not believe it! There were a lot of very talented musicians. I had felt very nervous when I'd started to play, but the further I played through the pieces, the more I enjoyed it.

I hadn't realised that there would be a final in Lockerbie, so the same rush of feelings passed through me then. Once all the performances were over, everyone gathered for the awards ceremony. Being announced the best in my discipline took me by surprise and I didn't want to have to play again in front of lots more people, but after I had played with the winners of the other disciplines, I felt that the singer who was presented with the Young Burnsian Of The Year Award was a very worthy winner!'

Joanna Stark, S2.

'Having been a member of the Madras wind band for a number of years, I have had the opportunity to play numerous styles of music spanning the genres; from the slammin' funk grooves of Stevie Wonder to the themes of iconic films such as The Magnificent Seven. Under Mrs Ruth Craib's unfaltering direction, the band has participated in countless events, including a tour to Holland and the Royal Highland Show, and has proved to be a truly rewarding experience on all counts.'

Tommy Alexander, drummer/percussionist, S5.

'Why direct The Rivals? Firstly, the challenge of the knotted, rather old fashioned language, making it roll easily off the tongue of the actors; secondly, the challenge and pleasure of trying a style of theatre in which the relationship between the actor and the audience is so important; and lastly it was lovely to indulge in the eighteenth century costumes, wigs and fans.

In this photograph Bob Acres on the left (*Jacob Scott*) is in Bath to try to charm Lydia Languish. She is not

remotely interested in him despite his best efforts to throw off his country bumpkin image and become a dandy. He has come to visit his good friend Captain Jack Absolute (*on the right of the photo, played by Max Chase*) to tell Jack about his longing for Lydia, while unbeknown to Bob Jack is himself romantically entangled with Lydia.'

Patricia Esler, Drama Teacher.

Eadie Manson from Adam Smith College and STV's The Hour show comes to Madras on a weekly basis to take the after school Junior Chefs club. The pupils from S1-3 make a variety of exotic and exciting dishes.

'The Madras pool needs constant maintenance. Here we have three Madras water babies checking to see if the drained pool has any sharp objects that need removing...with a little fun on the way!'

Malcolm Changleng, Principal Teacher (Curriculum), Physical Education.

'The water is your friend... you don't have to fight with water, just share the same spirit as the water, and it will help you move.'

Aleksandr Popov, former Olympic gold winning swimmer.

'I had never played lacrosse before I came to Madras. After some great PE lessons with Mr Changleng I feel my friends and I are ready to take on our local rivals St Leonards. Could this be the start of a fiery local derby?'

Tamara Levy, S4.

Prince William came to St Andrews in bleak February, and conquered Madras pupils with his charm. Did the girl in the centre with the mobile phone camera get the shot of her dreams?

'Who knew what to expect on that Friday Prince William and Kate Middleton visited their former university and home-town, St. Andrews? There were high anticipations which weren't let down as we got to see Kate and the future King walking down North Street.

We were greeted with a friendly handshake and some pleasant chat, leaving us all feeling proud to have met our future King and his wife.'

Zak Maas, S6 (directly in front of camera).

Jumping for joy at the arrival of Red Nose Day in March, the main method by which Comic Relief raises money for charity. It was founded in Britain in 1985 by the comedy scriptwriter Richard Curtis and comedian Lenny Henry in response to famine in Ethiopia. Since its inception it has raised over £650 million and the efforts of Madras pupils have helped to put food into the bowls of starving children, as well as staging a fun day in school.

A PORTRAIT OF

'I really enjoy the sporting activities at Madras because we work hard to improve our skills, but we play hard too. Bubble blowing is a favourite part of my curriculum!'

Maria Lahatskaya, S4.

Kate Watkins, Head of the Classics Department, and her Classics colleague *Andrew Lawrenson* brandish swords from Hadrian's Wall which they visit every June with 48 pupils from S1-S6. The shields were made by S1 pupils as part of their Roman Army Elective and the pupils holding them are Classics pupils in S5 and S6.

'A tradition begun in Madras College where senior students teach the younger ones is still alive today. As part of "World Book Day" *Rory Henretty (left) and Ryan McManus (right)* visited Kingsbarns primary school to share their favourite childhood stories with the pupils there.'

*E*mma Payne, English Department.

'This year first year pupils were offered the opportunity to take part in a project called Madras Paired Reading Club. It is a new initiative which aims to support pupils with their reading through peer learning. It follows a tried and tested method which has been refined over many years. Emphasis is placed on reading for understanding and enjoyment. This picture illustrates how the pupil and third year tutor talk about the text or book and build a rapport. The Paired Reading Club project is managed by teachers from the English and Support for Learning Departments and the school librarians.'

Jason Hynes, English Department.

'I am playing Lieutenant Roger Martins (*on left in photo*). He is a loud talking man who has worked his way up through the army over many years. He has a wife and two boys back home in England. He likes being in charge and issuing orders, but he also likes to have friendly talks with all the men in the army, to try to cheer newcomers up but also to try not to think about how he has left his family behind. Lt. Martins is well spoken and very formal when dealing with important matters to do with the war. I enjoy acting because you are able to leave yourself and inhabit other people's personalities.'

James Primmer, S3 Drama.

'I am playing Sergeant Frank McCafferty (*behind James*). The Sergeant is an extremely confident, self-assured leader. He is the sort of character who is admired for his determination and leadership skills. Frank left school with few qualifications and went straight into the armed forces at the age of 16. He says that joining the army was his one and only dream. I enjoy acting because it presents different challenges compared to other subjects. It gives pupils a chance to express themselves and really get involved. The play about the war in Afghanistan was created by the whole class and deals with the effects the conflict has on our society, as some of us have relatives fighting over there just now.'

Andrew Weir, S3 Drama.

'The Eco-Club has been in existence for three years and in that short time the members have managed to raise funds and build three large gardens where disused and overgrown areas once existed. As well as improving the outward appearance of the school, they have also been responsible for achieving international Eco-Schools status. We have won two internationally recognised awards in the space of three years. Both school sites have their own clubs but they work together on days like this, Eco-Action Day, which also happened on this occasion to be a successful Eco-Schools Inspection day! As well as planting a community orchard in nearby Stank's Park, and preparing the school's three new gardens, the school raised money for the Woodland Trust. Part of the Eco-Action day's activities involved welly whanging (throwing a welly as far as possible). That's why the three in the group: *James Primmer*, S3, Eco-Club chairperson; *Eleanor Linton*, S2, and *Mark Nicol*, S6, are pictured holding wellies.'

*B*rendan Fox, Eco-Schools Co-Ordinator.

The Course Fayre,
the first of its kind,
was run by both staff
and senior pupils to give
information about the
range of courses on offer.

'Although a slightly strange conversationalist, Count Dracula would strike those in his company as a rather charming and highly accommodating character. A foreign aristocrat, he receives his guest, the English estate agent Jonathon Harker, in his castle with great warmth. However, such amiability is a facade, masking the feral cravings for the taste of human blood, a facade that all too often wears thin. I enjoyed portraying this character as, having always been attracted to the dark side of the force, it gave me the opportunity to explore the sinister elements of human nature.'

Tommy Alexander, S5 Higher Drama, playing Dracula in Liz Lochhead's play.

'From the moment we stepped off the plane as part of the Ohio Exchange, my friends and I knew that we were in love with Scotland. Apart from all the attractions and landmarks, simply driving around the country was so beautiful and it was so green. It was wonderful to see all the old castles and stunning architecture. American buildings seem so much more sterile in comparison. Everyone we met through the Exchange made the trip truly unforgettable – it's crazy how spending just 20 days together with someone can make them like family. Madras itself had a laid-back, sociable atmosphere that I really enjoyed. The classroom experience differs slightly from the American style in curriculum structure; Madras is more like a university than a high school. My time in Scotland was amazing, and I plan on going back to visit as much as I can!'

A zalea Tang.

'The "Sew Arty" exhibition, staged in March 2011, was a showcase of art, craft and design produced by Creative Arts students and containing a selection of works from the Art, Home Economics and Craft and Technology departments of the school, with contributions from Music. The exhibition was open to the public and was a big success, demonstrating the wealth of talent within the school.'

Diane Houston,
Art & Design.

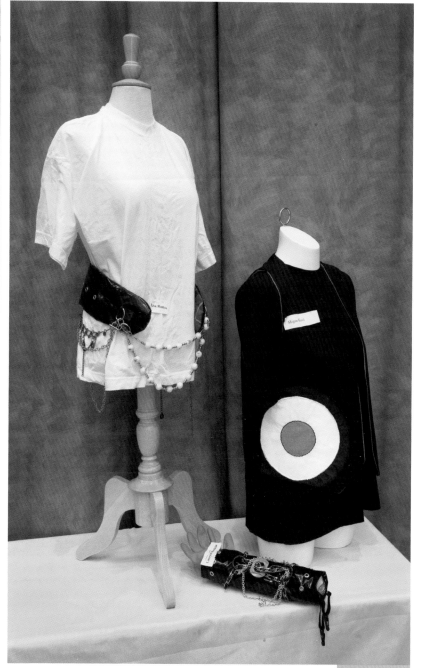

'I did actually land this gymnastics move on my feet. I was quite proud to gain so much elevation and keep my balance at the same time. It looks like I impressed my friend Cameron! The PE activities are really diverse and you have plenty of choice to try to build a healthy lifestyle. But I must say I do enjoy my gymnastics.'

Joseph Butchart, S3.

'The gym is one of my favourite learning areas because we do so many fun activities that really challenge you to do your best. I loved just hanging out with my friends (excuse the pun!) before we moved on to our gymnastics proper!'

Katie Lamb, S3.

'There were no extra curricular netball clubs in Madras when I joined the school four years ago. However, the commitment and natural talent of Madras College pupils made it easy for me to develop successful teams. Now over 60 pupils take part in the weekly training sessions and represent the school in regional and national competitions.

The girls' hard work and determination has led to a number of achievements and domination of the Fife Schools Netball Association Tournaments. Madras has held the S1 Tournament Title for three years and the S2 title for two years. For the last three years all of our teams have reached the quarter finals of the Scottish Cup.

I am extremely proud of all of the teams' achievements but I am even more proud of each individual girl's attitude and commitment to the team. They enjoy working hard and helping each other. It is great fun working with them and I am looking forward to the years to come.'

Lynsey Seeley, Physical Education.

'For me, football is just a game, not a drama.'

Michel Patini, former French football player, manager and current president of UEFA.

'The football team for me is extremely satisfying. Not only is it a fantastic opportunity to play in a team but there is also something special about scoring a goal in your team colours. The team skills I have learned here will stand me in good stead for the rest of my life. It's not at all totally serious though - practice is a place to socialise and have fun as well as play. The team even go as far as to take bets on how many times I will fall over in a match as I am the clumsiest person in the team!'

Courtney Gardiner, S5 (far right).

'On 10th March 2011 the Higher and Intermediate 2 Modern Studies class visited the Scottish Parliament in Edinburgh, as we had been studying devolved decision making in the Scottish Parliament. During our day's visit, we viewed Scottish politics in action as we received a tour around the Parliament, seeing inside MSPs' offices and conference rooms. We also witnessed First Minister's Question Time, and held MSP *Iain Smith* to account by asking him specific questions regarding the relationships between Westminster and Holyrood and the roles of MSPs and committees. Overall, our day's visit to the Parliament was a very enjoyable experience and helped us all to consolidate our newly learnt knowledge of the Scottish Parliament.'

Catriona Black, S5 (second, right).

Contemplating the seat of Scottish government: architectural masterpiece or monstrosity?

A PORTRAIT OF

Iain Smith, MSP, answers questions from Madras pupils.

The energetic staff of Craft & Technology, clockwise from left to right: *Colin Clark taking a swing; Jacqui MacGregor reading; Doug Walker kneeling; Stuart Kerrigan with rope and axe; Bill Kay with paddle; and Ken Duncan looking for his ball.*

'*Ryan* has made this clock as his final assessment piece for Intermediate 2 woodworking skills. This course is vocational for some learners who are aiming for craft-based apprenticeships and for others it allows a skill-based relief from paper work and exam preparation. This is one of the several diverse courses offered to senior pupils by Craft & Technology. Alongside this we offer academic courses in Graphic Communication, Conceptual and Applied Design as well as Engineering courses to Advanced Higher.'

Bill Kay, Craft & Technology.

'In the workshop we learned how to mix mortar, lay foundations, use plumb-lines and set the bedding between the bricks properly. We also learned how to build arches using a former. It was good when they didn't fall down.'

Thomas Green, S4 CC Skills pupil.

'A living room was built in the workshop for pupils to learn how to strip paint from walls, sand wooden frames, fill in holes and learn how to paint a house properly.'

Thomas Green, S4 CC Skills pupil.

A P O R T R A I T O F

181

Madras kayakers learn the skills of propulsion and staying upright from instructors from the University of St Andrews.

A P O R T R A I T O F

The Social Subjects team, teaching Geography, History and Modern Studies. *Sandra Thomson, Principal Teacher (Curriculum), stands in front of the map. Back row, left to right: Adam Smallwood; Paul Dagless; and Matthew Swift. In the front row are Paul Jones; John Clark; and Margaret Latto.*

'Going out to primary schools and chatting to the primary 7s about their move to the "big" school is one of the best parts of my job. We talked about classes, teachers, lunches, homework, clubs, the house system, sports and many other aspects of life at Madras College. It's great to see a group of pupils enthusiastic to make the transition and ready to contribute to the traditions and history of Madras.'

*K*enneth Wishart, *Principal Teacher of Guidance.*

Thumbs-up for the nuptials of Prince William and Kate from Madras supporters in the quad of St Salvator's College that unforgettable April day of blue skies and bonhomie. Note the patriotic headgear of the young lady in the second back row.

'Our group, Ramskeerie, had been performing for only a few months when we were given the opportunity to play at the Royal Wedding celebrations in the University of St Andrews Quadrangle. It was great playing in the main catering tent in front of a fluid audience of 2000!

Our set was the longest we had ever played and everyone seemed to enjoy our blend of Scottish traditional music. I hope there are more gigs like this one!'

Cameron Mackay, S5.

'The Great Assembly is a long running tradition of Madras College. Every year, two pupils give a "reflections" speech, looking back at their time as pupils of Madras College. From that terrifying first day when the third years give you wrong directions to class, to saying goodbye at the sixth year ball, it has certainly been a memorable journey. It is a time to acknowledge the people who helped us through, the teachers who went out of their way to run extra-curricular clubs and provide the support necessary to ensure the pupils have an ideal environment in which to develop into mature adults, ready to stand on their own two feet.'

Lindsay Wright and Miriam Malek, both S6, left to right in photograph.

'Set well back from the street, a suave Jacobean manor by William Burn, 1832-4.'

John Gifford, The Buildings of Scotland, Penguin Books, 1988.

'This was the first time I had tried hurdles as my Primary didn't have them. I loved it and was pleased to beat my friend Leah in this race (only by a whisper!). To make sports day, I had to come in the top four times. Unfortunately, I didn't make it but I am looking forward to next year's event as I wasn't far away.'

Louise Chaplain, S1 (on left).

'This year I took part in the Madras College Sports heats. As you can see in the picture above, I took part in the shot putt. Along with many others, I loved not only this event, but all the events the school had on offer from 800 metres to javelin. I'm sure everyone who took part had a great time!'

Amy Boxer, S3.

A PORTRAIT OF

A close-run race for S3 competitors. Is there a future Olympian here?

'I remember leapfrog from my younger days, a brilliant way to warm up for that morning's PE lesson.'

India Butler, S2.

'Each year group has a chance to enter all the athletic events and win points to become the overall boys or girls Silver Salver winner. I loved the field events, but track is my favourite. My abiding memory of this race was being so shook up by Mr Tarvet's starting gun that I had enough adrenalin to win the race. It was the loudest gun I had ever heard!'

Innes Little, S1.

Above: 'In 2008 I made my transition from primary school to secondary school which was to Madras College (Kilrymont Road). This was a huge change in my life, but I enjoyed every minute and I am looking forward to my final few years at South Street. In this photo many S3 pupils celebrated their last day at Kilrymont Road. It was a day with mixed emotions but I will remember all the fun times we had, including our S3 school trip which was a great experience.'

Michael Ferguson, S3.

Left: More S4 arrivals to South Street from Kilrymont Road.

'This was us preparing to go out on our Silver practice expedition. That weekend we were in the Glen Tilt area near Blair Atholl. The first day was long and tiring, but on the second weather was so bad that the rain was horizontal. No matter how miserable we were at times as we walked, it is great to think back that we succeeded and rose to the challenge.'

Fiona Paterson, in charge of Duke of Edinburgh Award, Madras College.

The Modern Languages Department proves its international worth with a banner. *Left to right: Catriona Harvey; Dorothy Orem (Principal Teacher 1); Lyn McCartney (Principal Teacher Curriculum Modern Languages); Dorothy Drylie; Colin Irving; Lesley Maix.*

'Higher French is a great subject. It is really good to learn about the culture as well as the language and it is a good qualification for university. It is my favourite subject and I intend to study it in S6.'

Heather Powrie, S5 (on right).

'Several Madras College pupils hosted French Exchange pupils from Poitiers, Loire Valley, in their homes for one week in June. This Exchange allowed the French to experience a totally different culture from what they would be used to at home and gave both parties a chance to try out the languages they have been learning in school. It was an enjoyable experience for all who were involved and both Scottish and French pupils were very sad to part at the end of the week.'

Cameron Mackay, S5.

A   P O R T R A I T   O F

'The Kiel Exchange was started as a result of correspondence between two historians, Dr John Thompson, who in 1955 had just become Rector of Madras College, and Professor Karl Dietrich Erdmann, Professor of Modern History at Kiel University. The Exchange has much to offer both on a linguistic and cultural level. Madras pupils who travel to Kiel stay with a host family, attend classes in school and take part in excursions. A former participant wrote: "The Kiel Exchange was one of the most exciting, fun, emotional, interesting, character building experiences of my life."

We hope that the Exchange will continue to thrive as it has clearly had an impact on around 1,500 German and Scottish families over the past five decades.'

– Dorothy Orem, Modern Languages, German.

'This banner was handmade by German pupils to commemorate the 25th anniversary of the Exchange programme between Madras College and Kieler Gelehrtenschule - an Exchange which is now in its 54th year and is the longest running school Exchange programme in the UK. Our Exchange not only proved to be an experience with countless hours of fun and laughter, but also one which has given us many fond memories and invaluable friendships. Our thanks go out to everyone whose efforts have kept the Exchange running for so many years, and made it such a memorable experience.'

Naomi Laing, S6 (right).

'My name is *Georg Rohardt* (*right*). I am 16 years old, from the German city of Kiel. St Andrews is very different from Kiel. In Kiel there are not that many old buildings. Kiel is bigger and focuses mainly on shipping. But let me tell you why I like St Andrews so much: in the last ten days I have become friends with many Scots and have learned a lot about Scotland. I have also tried Scottish country dancing and have enjoyed the Scottish weather! The only thing that keeps me from wanting to stay is my family and of course, my friends in Germany.'

Sisters of charity: *Amy Reid,* S3 (*right*) and her sister Ruth, S5 at a car boot sale to raise money for Namibia.

'Over 20 students at Madras agreed that a teaching experience of a lifetime to the sub-Saharan country of Namibia could definitely not be refused. Events in and out of the school such as quiz nights, fashion shows, car boot sales and coffee mornings raised some serious money to spend on resources for our three Namibian schools. At Shamangorwa some children walked 11 km to school for the 7 a.m. start. There was no canteen or running water so they had nothing to eat or drink until they returned home at night. Over 100 younger pupils, who were being taught in a classroom made out of sticks, or outside, often had no shoes and their thin torn clothes could not save them from shivering in the chilly mornings. Using our resources, we taught all ages a variety of subjects including English, Maths, Science, Geography and History. In PE lessons rounders was played and even Scottish country dancing taught. Working with the teachers and children of these Namibian schools has been life-changing and I am sure no one could ever forget. Hopefully this will be the start of a lasting relationship between Madras and the Namibian schools.'

Melanie Fleming, S6.

'Evening, weekend and holiday access to Madras College Community Use benefits all ages, enabling over 2800 local people to enjoy the wide ranging facilities and to take advantage of more than 140 classes, activities, groups and events.'

Andy Herd, Head of Community Use, Madras College.

'The photograph shows some of the members of the community drumkit class, led by me. We meet once a week throughout the winter months in Kilrymont School to master the skills of rock, swing, blues, waltz and cha-cha drumming. Although a recreational course, what is learned in class can be used by the students in their senior school music exams.'

Callum MacLeod,
Principal Teacher of
Expressive Arts, Waid
Academy, Anstruther.

'In the late 1970s the St. Andrews Angling Club formed a junior section to encourage the youth in the area to participate in the art of angling. Fortunately I was given the position of mentor to this group of twenty young people. I had been taught to tie flies by a professional tyer, Dunstan Hutchison, so to keep the interest of the young lads during the winter months I decided to hold weekly classes in Madras College Rugby Club Clubrooms, when it occupied the Victory Memorial Hall. Eventually we had to move up to the Kilrymont Road building of Madras College. Sadly, we have lost the youngsters who have all moved on, and there is no longer a junior section of the Angling Club. But the interest and skill in tying a fly which will catch a fish has never faded. The end product - the "perfect fly" - is the ultimate goal of the class.'

Keith Neilson, (second left) former pupil and teacher.

'I have been at Madras Community Use Dance since I was a toddler. I have taken all styles of dance: ballet, tap, Highland, jazz. Since passing all my dance exams I have now become a qualified dance teacher which is a great achievement for me, and I hope to pass on my knowledge and teaching skills to all the pupils hopefully I will be teaching in the near future.'

Kim Mcgrory, dedicated dancer.

'Pictured during an intensive indoor winter training session are the coaches and players from Largo CC junior section. The club contains many current Madras pupils (and FPs), together with youngsters from Madras associated primaries, who train hard at Madras during the winter and play both at Largo and the Madras playing fields at Station Park during the summer. Largo CC recruit from all over North East Fife and were awarded the Scottish Junior Club of the Year title in 2009. Amongst those pictured are Scotland Junior Internationals in both boys and girls cricket, together with an East Fife Sports Council "Coach of the Year"!'

Willie Anderson, (modest) cricket coach.

For years Fife maestro *Billy Anderson* (*centre*) has held an accordion tuition class in Kilrymont, under Community Use auspices. Members of *Billy's* class have gone on to form their own bands, having gained technical skill and confidence under his easy-paced tutoring. Note the line-up of ladies fingering the keyboards. Fiddlers are most welcome.

'The Dance Show is my favourite time of year. The weekend before we have rehearsals which is fun, except Carlyn shouts a lot, telling us to smile. Then the dress rehearsal is great when we have loads of photos taken in our fantastic costumes. We are always excited at the show to dance in front of hundreds of people - and we ALL remember to smile, so much so our faces hurt!'

Anna Davidson, age 9, P5.

The Summery Days

There is that buzz that hangs around,
When summer time is close
The tolls of winter are all but lost,
Already a whisper, a ghost.
As summer's breeze sweeps across the school,
Excitement sweeps the same way.
Pupils laze in the sun's bright glare
Throughout the long school day.

Waves of heat bring waves of content,
And silently we all agree
That a blaring sun means little work:
Always the Madrasian decree.
In classes pens doodle in a dreamy state,
Minds wander the lesson away,
For all teachers know the way it must go
Although no one would venture to say.

Any concentration is strictly forbidden
During such a heat.
The tint of a smile from that lazy vibe
Shadows everyone you meet.
The whole school groans with the weight of the year,
The desks and chairs feel worn out.
Everyone dreams in a dozy state
Of beaches and ice creams no doubt!

Hyper chat gurgles through the corridors,
Excitement is splurged through the classes
Swamped by the warmth of the summer feel,
That we savour as it passes.
Petals pattern the school lawn
As the year draws to a close,
Enjoying the summer while we still can
Because that's the way it goes.

Eilidh Northridge, S2.

MADRAS COLLEGE

'As Castle House and Vice Captains of 2011, (left to right) Lorna Willins, Peter Dennis, Catriona Black and Alex Sloan greatly look forward to proving that Castle really IS the House to be in! Throughout the year we will be helping and encouraging pupils, from first year through to sixth, in a variety of school activities and motivating them all to get behind Castle and win it for another year running! After all, Castle really is the fortress of Madras!'

A PORTRAIT OF

'Blackfriars has always prided itself on its strong Scottish spirit, on never giving up. Blackfriars is also the House where it is important to be yourself and do the very best at what you can as an individual. This is the attitude that the House Captains of 2011 (*left to right: Neil Pexton; Bryony Drummond; Hannah Basten; Max Chase*) hope to inspire. Blackfriars hopes to be a unified House, and despite not winning the House Championship in previous years, just like the Scots we never give up. This year could be the year!'

ax Chase, S6.

left to right: 'Kirsty Duncan (*Female Vice-Captain*), Rory Henretty (*Male Captain*), Anna Zaitseva (*Female Captain*) and Tony Kestner (*Male Vice-Captain*) are pictured at the Cathedral's Priory building which has been traditionally identified as the residence of the Prior, the head of the cathedral Priory. The Priory Captaincy team prides itself on punctuality and attendance at all House events, not least the House assemblies. We are hoping to secure the House Championship this year and are confident that we will with our strong leadership and great team of prefects.'

Rory Henretty, S6.

'Playing volleyball at West Sands for PE was great. It was so much better to be outside in the fresh air on the beach than in the cramped gym hall. Playing an enjoyable sport with my friends wasn't just good exercise - we learned a lot about volleyball, and got a suntan too!'

Flora Chirnside (front), S3.

'The contrast between now and hundreds of years ago is incredible. Playing sport on an area of land used for executions really makes you think about what the past was like for the people of St. Andrews. But now those times have gone and to be playing volleyball in front of the Blackfriars Chapel is something special. Our school is not only privileged with these historic landmarks, but with fantastic opportunities to play volleyball and other sports that some schools may not have the chance to play. Some things never change though: Calum Willison's digs making everyone laugh; how competitive Fraser Hayles gets; the sheer campness of Ben Kinsley's serve; and Liam Carson being the best in class. He thinks that!'

Ben Kinsley, S5.

'Although we play lots of golf competitions outside school, we really enjoy trying to win the many ancient cups that Madras golfers can play for. The oldest trophy is made of melted-down rupees and dates from the 1850s. Wow! We are really competitive on the course...you should see the Jock Hutcheson Trophy - it's massive! The photograph was taken on the Eden Links course while competing for this trophy.'

Chris Fleming S2; Sean Cowan S3; Kyle Ferguson S2.

'The moment they had been waiting for, they had spent hours pouting, preening and polishing for this - and that was just the guys.'
Caitlin Paterson, S6.

A PORTRAIT OF

Congratulations Class of 2005

Proud prize-winners show off their achievements.

'Madras College has been my home for six years now, and it's hard to believe it's over. I cannot think of a better way to mark the end of my time here than to be the recipient of such a prestigious award. The Science Dux was something I had always aspired to, but never quite expected to become reality - much like my ambition to become a veterinary surgeon. To be awarded not only Science Dux, but also Dux of the school, and to have been accepted by Edinburgh Vet School was a dream come true. I think this is an example of what any person can achieve under the right conditions - good teachers, supportive friends and parents and commitment of the individual. I don't know of another school which would have let me undertake five Advanced Highers this year.'

Lindsay Wright (left), S6.

'Winning the Arts Dux still hasn't quite sunk in; the acknowledgment, the recognition, and most importantly the medal! If I'd known back in first year (when Arts involved making posters about the days of the week in German, and imaginary newspaper articles in English) that six years of essays, verb endings and sometimes frustrating Latin translations would lead not only to such an impressive award, but also to a university place and ultimately to so much enjoyment...well, I don't think I would have believed it.'

Alice Rhodes (right), S6.

'While there has been a piping class at Madras College since 1953, the Pipe Band was only formed in 1993, the idea of *Alan McGeogh*, Principal Teacher of Music at the time. It was a small Band at first, but was soon popular enough to be asked to perform at a number of events each year.

Pipe Major *Bert Barron* became piping instructor in 1953. In 1994 his son *Roderick* took over the piping tuition. *Roddy* is still teaching at the College, with assistance from piper *Andy Soutar,* and drummers *Stuart Foggo* and *Naomi Thom*. Around 70 pupils are currently learning pipes and drums and the Band now regularly performs with twelve to sixteen pipers and up to twelve drummers. Thanks to generous donations they now have new uniforms, including kilts made with their own specially designed Madras College tartan, which is in the Scottish Register of Tartans.

The Band is now in great demand to perform at various annual events, including the Midsummer Charity Ball and St Andrews Day Torchlit Procession.'

Lorna Talbot, events coordinator, keeper of the Pipe Band's kilt outfits, and reserve piper.

A P O R T R A I T O F

'One of the best things about the South Street building is the chance to escape the confines of the classroom and grab a moment to relax. As the year progresses, the pressure to maintain a good grade and complete work can be extremely demanding, and more than once my friends have had to bear the brunt of my ranting – much to their disdain. Therefore, on the rare occasion that the sun does actually shine, it's great to have some time to just unwind and fortunately the school grounds are able to grant us that brief respite just when we need it.'

Catherine Macrae, (sitting right) S6.

'No wonder I got off to a quick start; Mr Tarvet the chief starter almost shot me! This was my 200m race which I won and which put me en route to the S2 boys Individual Cup. Yes!'

Stanley Ho, S2, competing for Castle House.

A PORTRAIT OF

'I was delighted to do my bit for Blackfriars as I was this year's House Captain! I was pleased to qualify for so many events but gutted that we were last in the chase for the cup.'

*F*inlay Jones, S5, competing for Blackfriars House.

'In this tense Inter-House relay I was determined to be in front on the first leg so that Priory could beat Castle and Blackfriars. I was hoping that my face didn't look funny when I ran (but, obviously, it did!). My first Sports Day at Madras was very memorable and I hope to do well in the years to come.'

Ellenor Waddell (on right),
winner of 2011 S1 Girls' Cup.

A P O R T R A I T O F

'I really enjoyed being chosen to represent my House on sports day. It is a great experience and loads of fun. PS: I won the race!'

*M*orven Smith (with baton), S3, competing for Blackfriars House.

'It felt so wonderful to win because there was real competition in this race and it went to the wire. I loved winning House points for Priory and was chuffed we won the Sports Cup.'

Daniel Duthie, S2, competing for Priory House.

MADRAS stories

'When I began teaching in 1955, I was fortunate to be employed initially as an itinerant teacher of Physical Education - in other words "the visiting gymie". Tayport, Newport, Newburgh, St. Andrews Burgh, Madras College and Bell-Baxter were my designated schools. Most had Primary Departments and up to 3rd year pupils and were known as Junior Secondaries.

This was a wonderful introduction to teaching, giving me opportunities to gain knowledge and experience teaching across the whole spectrum - the youngest to the oldest. This helped me to prepare pupils in their progression from primary to the larger secondary schools of Bell Baxter and Madras College.

As Depute Principal of Madras College I had to ensure the pitches were playable and that buses left on time. I had to wait for visiting teams to arrive and to referee at least one game. To see all the pupils smartly dressed in school uniform, either leaving St. Andrews or waiting for their opponents to arrive, made one proud to belong to Madras College.'

Keith Neilson, *former pupil and teacher.*

'My first day at Madras Primary (next to the South Street building) at the Easter intake I cried so much mother was told: "bring him back in 6 months". I was last in the class until P7 when Mrs Smith frightened me, just in time to pass my eleven plus exam. At primary school I got four of the belt from Dr McLeod, rector of the "big school", for teasing a girl.

We were the first pupils to use the new building ("The Old Order Changeth"). Madras for me was sport, guided quietly by Tom Croll. Although a Prefect and then Head Boy, it was Athletics Captain and Rugby Vice-Captain which gave me satisfaction. My time of 1m 57.6secs for 880 yards representing Scottish Schools has not been bettered in 50 years. Rector Dr Thompson was also the careers advisor and guided me to Aberdeen University to do a BSc in Agriculture.

Coming back home to farm kept me close to Madras. My three daughters were all Hockey Captains at Madras, with the eldest playing for Scotland and then Great Britain in the World Student Games. One, who was Science Dux, went to Cambridge to do Maths; another went to Oxford to do Maths; the third went to Bedford to do PE and Art – the result of a good Madras education!

While my girls were at Madras I was on the School Board and Chairman of the PTA. My link with Madras is still strong as I am Chairman of the Madras College Endowment Trust.

Madras is the only school I have known. My life is the only life I have known. There is no doubt Madras College has influenced many parts of my life!'

Colin Mitchell, Madras Primary 1948 – 1955;
Madras College 1955 – 1961.

'School life is an awkward, anxious, hopeful and, often, hilarious time. I wasn't a particularly good student when I was at Madras in the 1990s – my concentration and focus were always wavering. Despite this, I have some very significant memories, and the scenes from those days are particularly nostalgic.

My fondest memories take place in history classes. Mr Casey was a strict teacher who demanded respect, hard work and maturity. His classes were intense, but part of the intensity came from the stories he told. There were no textbooks, gimmicks, or media to capture our young minds - his presence was enough to command our attention. He usually sat at the front and his voice was rarely loud; he told us stories about changing lives, dark times and discoveries. We listened for the detail that we needed to know for Mr Casey's questions and our tests, but we listened because it was new, sometimes disturbing and sometimes satirical. The most poignant tale was that of the Somme. I recently read "Birdsong" and the horror of that battle took me back to the day Mr Casey told us about the carnage. I remember him saying that he lost family in that battle and it all seemed so horribly real.

Other scenes stand out too. There was the walk to and from school through the Lade Braes; the legendary snow week, where South Street and classes were frozen out of commission; having teachers that still dressed as gentlemen in bow ties; walking past Blackfriars Chapel to get to registration and not thinking anything of it; thinking that a v-necked jumper as part of a uniform was grossly unjust; Mr Lindsay reading Chaucer as a woman, adopting a jumper as a wimple; turning the Home Economics classroom into one gigantic spider web when the teacher popped out of the room for two minutes; and the endless mucking about.

As a high school teacher, I'm constantly united with memories while watching pupils progress through adolescence. I now understand the pressure of delivering a curriculum and how plotting and capering hinder your plans. I look back with an inkling of shame whilst thinking of how much of a pest I sometimes was. However, I also look back and appreciate how important fun and silliness are in creating a unique time.'

Hayley Dalrymple, pupil, 1991-97.

'Those first steps off the bus into the epic expanse of the grounds of Kilrymont are filled with trepidation. Seemingly endless numbers of unknown faces smile, snarl and shout and laugh as new recruits wander uncertain towards their lives. Should I go in that door or stay out? If I choose to go in, what will I find? Who is that? Where are they from? What am I supposed to do now? The older pupils serenely make their way to wherever in the labyrinthine corridors that they're headed. Happily, for me at least, your new life is thrown at you at breakneck speed. Registration, schedules, plans, maps, names, subjects.

But first you must negotiate the teachers, some of whose names were already legend for those of us lucky enough to have had siblings treading the ground before us. My older sister would utter names as if to haunt, calling others who would inspire.

Casey (History): Fear and awe in more than equal measure.

Mackay (English): Inspiration and enthusiasm unbounded.

Malcolm (Science): Raconteur and rebel.

Galloway (The Rector): Peerlessly stalking the corridors as if from another age.

I think, however, it was out-with the confines of the classroom that I got the most of my time from Madras. On hand were the coaches and enthusiasts for school sport. I don't think any of us, the same group through the years, who formed the backbone of school rugby teams, ever quite appreciated how lucky we were to have the Tarvets, the Trewarthas and the Ronaldsons of the PE department. They would sacrifice their own time and effort to turn us into a pretty capable team.

By asking pupils who are fourteen or fifteen to be part of the 'system' as Prefects in 3rd year lets those pupils know that when you move up – the first growing up part is done. By giving those pupils the responsibility of being part of the greater St.Andrews community in South Street, you grow up for a second time.

I think the greatest compliment I can pay my time to Madras is that those people I grew up with are still very much part of my life. We have seen each other graduate, work, marry, have children and we still reminisce at the quirks of Mr Harkins' physics lessons or Mr Mole on a motorbike. Many of these names will be forgotten or unknown by the current crop stepping off those buses at Kilrymont but for me, they are legend.'

Nick Rougvie, Madras pupil, 1989-95: former broadcaster; Head of Public Relations and Media Operations, Scottish Rugby.

'Primary school aside, Madras College is really where it all began for me. The Kilrymont and South Street buildings provided me with an environment and space for trial and error. Within these walls, I have had the privilege of creating and nurturing meaningful friendships and relationships, and the support and time to grow into a more mature individual. When I remember Madras, I think about the endless academic and extra-curricular opportunities I was presented with: various music activities; school concerts; prize-giving; sports days. In spite of the split-site nature of the school, there was a real sense of community, pride and achievement. I carried that feeling with me to Cambridge University. I believe Madras has taught me that if we invest in our pupils, they can aspire to constantly achieve bigger and better things, as I tried to and as I have.'

Natasha Yapp, Madras pupil, 2002-08.

'The bicycle was a complete surprise and delight, presented to me at the S6 Ball in April 2007. With its school badge and safety lights flashing and blinking I managed to ride it in my kilt for a few yards around the Hall, breaking my own "no cycling in school" rule to great amusement. For weeks before this event S6 pupil Grace Carradice whose speciality was Technology had laboured in any hours and minutes she could find to build the bike from parts given or scavenged, and had wired it up with various electronic gizmos for my greater safety and visibility. Her teacher Mr Bill Kay had also, I believe, helped with the project. Grace has since graduated with First Class Honours in Technology from Liverpool University.'

Lindsay Matheson, former Rector.

A pride of Madras Rectors, left to right: Ian Gilroy (1975-85); David Galloway (1985-97); Ian Jones (2007 -); Lindsay Matheson (1997-2007). The mathematically minded reader may wish to add up the number of years of service between them. Sadly Dr Gilroy passed away in September 2011.

Madras College Archive

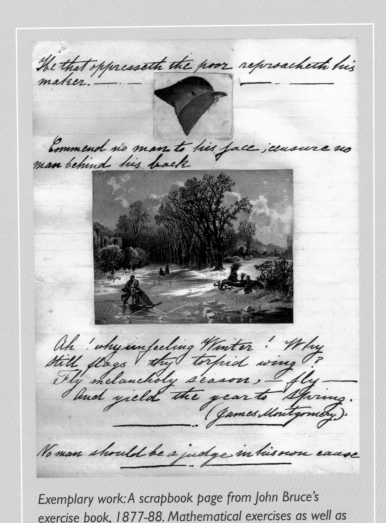

Exemplary work: A scrapbook page from John Bruce's exercise book, 1877-88. Mathematical exercises as well as artistic expression came with equal ease to this gifted pupil.

'This is my account of how the Madras College Archive has developed during the last three or four years. It has long been known that the school possesses many interesting items that illustrate our past. There are over 7000 items of various sorts that have been retained since the foundation of the school in 1833. Until the 1990s, however, there was no catalogue of any sort, and the items - mostly books, papers, logs, photographs, magazines and trophies - were not seen as a formal archive. Mr Galloway (rector 1985-97) had commissioned the first catalogue and stored many archive items in A2 document boxes in a small room on the third floor of what is now the Music House. This was distinct progress although the location was cold, remote and unsuitable for constructive archive work. During session 2007-08 two senior boys, Matthew Wright and Hamish Kinnear, used some of the available resources to write several articles of interest, published in "The Citizen". Following a meeting with the new rector Mr Jones I agreed to take on the task of reorganising the archive and formed a small working group that included Matthew and Hamish who by this time had left school but who worked throughout the summer to start the reorganisation of the resources.

In September 2008 I convened an inaugural meeting of the Archive Support Group comprising teachers, pupils, former teachers and former pupils, with additional support and advice willingly given by Dr Reid the senior archivist of St Andrews University. The objectives we set were to create a modern catalogue following current accepted archive practice, to make the resources as widely accessible as possible and to set up a system of responding to enquiries from outside. We divided the support group into sub-groups to tackle these tasks.

By 2011 our Archive Support Group had achieved the following: All the items have been re-catalogued, initially in paper form and then electronically. Over

The Modern Schoolgirl

'"Cynicus" was the name adopted by former Madras College pupil Martin Anderson (1854-1932) for his work as artist, humorist, and illustrator. The son of the stationmaster at Leuchars, he made quite a name for himself throughout Britain in the colour postcard business, setting up the Cynicus Publishing Company in Tayport. This illustration gives a clue to his style, letting us judge whether the modern schoolgirl at the turn of the century was entirely happy with her academic school curriculum. If we also had one about the "modern schoolboy" we might better be able to judge his social politics!'

Lindsay Matheson, former Rector.

the summer of 2009 two other senior pupils who had just left, Jamie Murphy and Michael Greig, assisted greatly in the process of re-boxing all the paper, book and magazine materials in A4 boxes kindly donated by the university. Maia Sheridan, one of the university archivists, trained the pupils for their task and Liz Higgins, the school Librarian, oversaw the work. The entire archive has been relocated in a ground-floor cupboard (beside Room K3) which was generously provided by the Social Subjects department. An archive website (www.madrascollegearchive.org.uk) has been created by Arlen Pardoe, who commenced the formidable task of scanning and making available on this website large sections of the most interesting holdings. The Responses Group, with Arlen Pardoe's assistance, developed a formal on-line registration process for all email contacts, enabling enquiries to be handled efficiently.

A former pupils' hockey team of 1905, formidable unsmiling opponents ready to clash sticks with all-comers despite the pose of gentility.

The 1937-38 1st Rugby XV, undefeated in 18 matches, pictured in the quad with coach J.C. Caldwell and Rector J.D. McPetrie. Back row right is Bob Scott, later capped for Scotland.

Christine Noble (former Administrative Coordinator) has catalogued the 170 trophies held by the school, a hundred of which are used within the current Awards system. Many new items have been added to the archive, particularly through the generosity and enthusiasm of FPs Frances Humphries, Anne Morris and Edmund Robertson. Talks and displays illustrated by some of the artefacts have been given by me to Dundee University, the Madras FP Girls' Club and the St Andrews Preservation Trust.

A group led by Mr Galloway and Mr Hodge has created a separate resource containing as much information as could be found about the history of the Burgh School (1889-1963). Work has begun by pupils in the English Department to interview former pupils and teachers for a file of Oral History. Support has been given to a recently-retired FP in Leicestershire, Ken Paterson, who has produced a 150-page book containing the known details about the 74 former pupils who gave their lives in WW1 and WW2.

The Under 14 football team, with the coveted shield, won when they became Scottish Champions at Hampden Park in 1993, pictured at Kilrymont with coach Harvey Munn and Depute Rector Lyn Brown. They wear new strips donated by James River GB Papers.

Gary Adamson, Madrascals Player of the Year in 1980, photographed with Scottish International rugby player Finlay Calder, who is holding a pet lion, having been selected to play for the Scottish Lions.

"Isle of Light: St Andrews: 6th & 7th Feb: 1914.

The performances of the new comic opera, "The Isle of Light," in the Town Hall on 6th and 7th February by the Madras College pupils, were artistically and otherwise a great success. On Friday and Saturday evenings, and on Saturday afternoon, the hall was crowded with delighted audiences.

"The Isle of Light" is admirably suited for young people. The very title is suggestive of a romantic world, and it is a delightful arcadian island which is the scene of the story. This island has perpetual sunshine by day and peculiar laws against the use of artificial lighting and heating.

From the Madras College Magazine of April 1914, poignant reminder of the words attributed to Sir Edward Grey, the Foreign Secretary, a matter of months later on the outbreak of the First World War: 'The lamps are going out all over Europe, we shall not see them lit again in our lifetime.'

Work continues on many other aspects, including the biographies of former staff, and a system of retention of current Madras College items of interest is being developed, so that in the future it will be possible to find out more about day-to-day school life in days gone by. In session 2010-11 an illustrated description of a year in the life of the school is being produced by a local author and a local photographer. Although much still remains to be done we feel that in the last three years considerable progress has been made towards our goals of organising the resources and making them widely accessible to all who may be interested.'

Lindsay Matheson, chairman of the Archive Support Group and former Rector, Madras College (1997-2007).

Additional assitance from Arlen Pardoe.

Clockwise from top:

A tinted Victorian etching of pupils of various ages enjoying the front lawn during free time.

Ad hoc guitar group The Dominies (Messrs Edwards, Smart and Lindsay) at a school social in 1977.

A mixed group of staff and pupils taken at the annual S6 Ball in 1995.

Senior pupil David Sinclair receives a national award from the Scottish Mathematical Association in 1982.

The Second Door

A hushed silence emanated from the centre of the room as the spotlights switched on. Pillars of light illuminated the obscure facade tearing the darkness away and revealing row on row of highly polished glass panels sculpted into the shape of a rippling wave. A melodic tone permeated the thick night air followed by a soft, soothing voice: 'On behalf of the Aflux organization I am pleased to announce that 2098 is the start of a new era. An era of joint partnership between ourselves, a leading technological development firm and the education division of the Fife Council. It is with pleasure that I announce the brand new Madras College multi-purpose school officially open.' The crowd erupted in spontaneous applause as a pair of iron bolted doors at the base of the artificial cliff slowly opened - a gaping mouth of darkness leading to another world. As the praise subsided the crowd filed through the portal in strict order, their faces grinning like small children at Christmas, but with eyes blank and emotionless as empty holes.

I walked down the corridor trying not to think about the people whose presence I was in, or what they might think of me. But, as the procession proceeded I felt more and more out of place. Furtive glances were being cast in my direction every time I looked up to admire the multi-faceted ceiling and I felt a sure certainty that the two people behind me were staring at the back of my neck. Their cold breaths were sending shivers up my spine. Was it possible that they could tell that I was intruding from another place and time? Surely I wasn't that conspicuous. Dwelling on it no further I bent down to tie my shoelace, a bead of salty fear appeared on my forehead as half the crowd looked down at me condescendingly, judging me with those blank eyes. They smirked in unison and walked off. Both angry and relieved, I got up and tried to open the door immediately on the left. The door gave way under the lightest touch and I stood inside the classroom. My eyes widened and pulse raced at what I saw. The room was divided into cubicle-spaces, one for each pupil. Within the small rooms the walls, floor and ceiling were covered by a massive LED touch-sensitive display. Tentatively I touched one of the walls which immediately turned a pleasant blue colour. A low pitched whirring sounded from the front of the classroom. It became louder and louder. I glanced out of the cubicle and standing right in front of me was a small one metre high robot. Seeing me it issued the statement: 'Remain within your cubicle until the end of the school day.' As it entered, the same soft, soothing tone emanated from the speakers 'Welcome to your new classroom, you have been assigned cubicle number 101. The cubicle will guide you through different subjects for the entire day. Lunch will be provided by me at twelve o'clock…' Rather disinterested by this monologue, I gave the cubicle a proper inspection. There was nothing to be seen other than the blue screen, which was rather disappointing, so I walked out to the front of the classroom. This seemed to distress the small robot significantly as it stood in the same place clicking, whirring and at random intervals stating the single word 'twelve.' Looking around I tried to find an off switch to put it out of its misery. Hidden behind a small flap on the wall I found an invitingly yellow button which I proceeded to press.

The moment I touched it the room crumpled into complete oblivion. Reality decided to take a holiday and I was left in complete darkness, unable to see, hear or feel anything at all. A bright red beam of light appeared, engulfing me and giving my skin an unnatural sheen. I gazed up at the unbearably bright source and the beam intensified. I felt something in the pit of my stomach lurch as my whole body seemed to be transfixed by the light, moving up as if it were escaping through my pupils. Feeling faint, I closed my eyes and succumbed to darkness. The lone figure stood for some time with closed eyes in a world of darkness, overwhelmed by the red beam of light. As the red slowly faded and was replaced by a pleasant shade of blue, the eyes flickered open, revealing blank, empty emotionless pits. A faint smirk passed over the face as the figure walked off into darkness.

I opened my eyes and took off the pair of glasses I had been wearing. Wiping a greasy smear from the front of the lenses, I listened to the Fife Council representative: 'I hope you have enjoyed the short glimpse into the future provided by our new 3D visualization system and that we have your new school finished and ready to use within the next ten years.' Walking into the quad, I embraced the fresh spring air, happy to be back at the old Madras College and trying to remember what had exactly happened over the past fifty minutes.

Submission by Andrei Ruskuc (S4) for the Nichola Johnston Prize, in memory of a Madras pupil who died of cystic fibrosis. The bravest of the brave, Nicky started Madras on 22nd August 2000. She passed away on 22nd March 2004 when she was in her 4th year. She would have been 16 years of age on 25th May of that year.

Hero of the playground

He closed his eyes and remembered the heat of the sun baking his back as he subconsciously listened to the idle chatter of the excitable pupils enjoying June's midday sun. He remembered the refreshingly cool, rough feel of the pillar against his cheek while he puzzled over his friend's words; 'Think of the glory old chap! Think of... the honour.'

As his eyes flickered open once more, he was greeted by a cacophony of sound that engulfed this tranquil memory and replaced it with fear, confusion and above all, excruciating pain. He glanced down at his uniform and saw thick, congealing blood bubble out of his abdomen and ooze into the muddy mire of No-Man's Land. There was nothing glorious, nothing honourable about this; no man's suffering should be applauded or wished; to die in a pitiful foxhole does not make you a better person. He pushed up with all the strength left in him up onto his knees and fumbled on the sodden ground for his rifle. His filthy, callused hands eventually grasped the cold metal steel of his weapon just as he heard a tremendous crack and felt a terrible burning in his chest. Falling to the ground once more, he felt the burning spread throughout his body like wild fire and so he sank back into his muddy grave.

A sudden chatter of merciless gunfire filled the air with screams of agony and sent him drifting back to that baking sun, that idle chatter, cloistered by the grand pillars that protected the quadrangle. Again he was the carefree, light-hearted student; 'hero of the playground' resounded through his mind, ricocheting round the quad's walls.

Strolling through the flagstoned courtyard; washed-out memories flitted in an out of sight; The Rector, Mr McKenzie, proudly marching the corridors with his long black robe billowing behind him; the rugby team swaggering out into the quad bursting with exuberance; the rich, enticing smell from Mrs Louden's cookery class constantly gnawing at a boy's hunger, tempting you down into the kitchens. The old, limping janitor, who would never leave a window pane dusty or a scuttle empty. He remembered sitting in the Rector's office, waiting for his first trophy and inspecting the portrait of Andrew Bell, who looked down at him with stern, expectant eyes.

Most vivid of all was the spectacular recruiting army rallies; banners flying, pristine uniforms, boots that shone as brightly as the faces of the onlooking pupils. Then the gruff recruiting sergeant bearing down on him like some hungry wolf, eager for young meat and his friends, all too willing to be snatched away. He saw the younger pupils staring in awe as the older chaps signed their lives away. That was the day he left

Madras, the day life became a constant struggle against the unrelenting current that swept him all the way to the water-logged fields of Belgium.

A warm hand clutched his shoulder and sent him firing back into a world of suffering. His eyes, gritty and bloodshot, scrutinized the surroundings only to find layers of corpses fogged by acrid smoke and a lonely white rag wearily waving at the opposite side of field. A shot of anger pulsed through his veins; countless lives lost, unbearable suffering for a glorified bog and a white rag.

Then imperceptibly the anger was replaced by a cold chill that seeped through him very slowly, leaving him with a single solitary thought; the great horse chestnut tree that he had once loved to gaze at; standing like a king; towering above its subjects, bowing to no one. No howling wind, no biting cold could diminish its power. It would forever stand tall and proud.

And as the last wisps of life left him he smiled and once more pondered on that beautiful midday sun.

In memory of Logan Studley; a Madras pupil who died in Belgium.

Submission by Geir Darge (S4) for the Nichola Johnston Prize.

The Late 2nd Lieut. LOGAN STUDLEY,
East Yorkshire Regiment.

The Exam

Jolted out of my trouble-free dreams by a shrill ringing, I stumbled out of my cosy duvet-nest and fumbled for the switch on the side of the hellish contraption. I stood on the spot for a minute, slowly blinking and fighting the urge to crawl back into the warmth of my bed and drift off far away from anything associated with cold, tiredness and school. Ugh, school that week meant exams, which intensified the urge to sleep, to forget. I glanced at the scribbly mess of paper and pen that was pinned to my wall. Maths. Well, there went my enthusiasm. Nevertheless, I began my preparation for school and had my breakfast which was practically shoved down my gullet by my "loving" parents. Nothing like nausea first thing in the morning.

I could feel the seconds tick by as the merciless chasm of Credit Maths - Paper 2 - drew ever closer. A bell similar to that which had awoken me that morning rang suddenly, causing me to start. Helped along by a sudden wave of people, I made my way to the mass gathering outside the hall. A friend frantically chatted - to me or herself, I haven't a clue - about pacing yourself and being calm, all the while amassing five pencils, a ruler, a protractor, rubber, sharpener, calculator, highlighters and compass into her seemingly bottomless pencil case. I inwardly raised my eyebrows and allowed myself a small smirk as I double-checked that my pen and calculator were still in my back pocket. Looking around at all the chatting, panicky-but-(mostly)-trying-not-to-show-it faces that surrounded me, which no doubt matched my own, I noticed a group of people all with revision books out, frantically flicking through them. I was pleased with the amount of revision I had done, although I silently prayed that there would be nothing about box plots, whatever they were…Doors opened, the atmosphere drained to leave only tension as thick as treacle and the flutter of a million butterflies as they somehow materialised into people's stomachs. A buzz of low murmuring caused the air to tickle my ears as we poured into the hall and fought for tables close to friends, or at least, someone we knew.

As I tried to make myself comfortable in the rickety, old, wooden chair behind the desk I'd chosen, I was struck by how, interestingly, the acoustics of the room were so that the teachers' footsteps echoed menacingly and the faintest whisper could be heard from across the room. Just an amazing coincidence, I guess. As a teacher droned on in a monotone about something or other, I can't really remember (It mustn't have been important) I yawned and got a mouthful of the perfume that the girl in front of me had just sprayed, missing herself completely. My eyes watered and I felt increasingly nauseous as I tried, and failed, to get the skunk-worthy taste out of my mouth by drinking almost all of the water I had. Great, now I was either going to die of thirst or need the bathroom halfway through the exam. Knowing my luck, it would be the latter. The teacher finished speaking and there was a wave of noise as everyone simultaneously turned their pages.

Ten minutes into the paper, I was bombarded by a succession of questions causing me to curse my teacher (well, how else was it alien to me?) and my brain's memory capacity. Deciding to return to them later, I tried another, only this time my calculator wouldn't work. Frustrated, as I knew how to do it, I sat and tried every combination under the sun to try and bypass the accursed syntax error, without success. Exhaling, I looked up and almost fell out of my uncomfortable chair. I had less than half an hour to finish the entire paper. Not caring about the quality of my handwriting, I rushed through the paper, checking the clock every spare second and growing anxious at the increasing number of people seemingly finished. On the last question a teacher selected me as their next victim to unsettle. I immediately stopped writing and waited for them to move on, only they didn't. Without lifting my head, I glanced at the clock. Five minutes. I counted the seconds as they stood there, waiting for god knows what, and wondered how accidental it would seem if I were to shift my chair

slightly and possibly crush a toe or three. After they finally prised their clumpy feet from the floor behind me and moved away from me, I hurriedly finished the paper and pushed it away from me as if it were dangerous to my health, which it probably was.

Leaving the hall, I felt my eyes begin to sting. Cursing under my breath, I quickly removed the evidence that I had been felled by some black ink and a few sheets of paper, and glanced around me that no-one had witnessed it. I knew my stressed-out, over-active brain was making mountains out of molehills, but I couldn't help but feel slightly (ok, hugely) worried at the thought of my expectant parents finding out the marks I got, which would no doubt be horrific. Feeling deflated, I recovered my bag from the reducing pile and made my way to my next class, squirreling the troublesome thought into the furthermost reaches of my subconscious to be dealt with afterwards, maybe never.

Zoë Davies, S3, winner of the Nichola Johnston Prize.